THE P

There was once a liv
who made himself
pockets and gave himself the stage name of Pochetto.
He was the first Pochetto, but over the years there
have been many many more – Pochetto the jester,
Pochetto the clown who lost his laughter, and
Pochetto the maker of a thousand sounds.

Patrick, the latest in the long series of Pochettos,
comes to work in the same circus as Sam, a lonely
little girl who wants to be a clown and who loves
to hear stories about the earlier Pochettos.

This is a haunting collection of fable-like stories
which, like the fairy tales of Oscar Wilde, will be
treasured by children and adults alike.

Commended in the 1979 Australian Children's Book
of the Year Award.

TED GREENWOOD

The Pochetto Coat

Illustrated by Ron Brooks

PUFFIN BOOKS

Puffin Books, Penguin Books Australia Ltd,
487 Maroondah Highway, P.O. Box 257
Ringwood, Victoria, 3134, Australia
Penguin Books Ltd,
Harmondsworth, Middlesex, England
Penguin Books,
625 Madison Avenue, New York, N.Y. 10022, U.S.A.
Penguin Books Canada Ltd,
2801 John Street, Markham, Ontario, Canada
Penguin Books (N.Z.) Ltd,
182-190 Wairau Road, Auckland 10, New Zealand

First published by Hutchinson Group (Australia) Pty Ltd, 1978
Published in Puffin Books, 1981
Copyright © Ted Greenwood, 1978
Illustrations copyright © Ron Brooks, 1978

Offset from the Hutchinson hardback edition.
Made and printed in Hong Kong by
Wah Cheong Printing Press Ltd

CIP

Greenwood, Ted, 1930-
The Pochetto coat.

First published: Richmond, Vic.: Hutchinson of
Australia, 1978.
For children.
ISBN 0 14 031475 X.

I. Brooks, Ron, 1948- II. Title.

A823'.3

Contents

Contents

PROLOGUE: POCHETTO

Why hello there.

Hello.

Come on, you can come right on in if you want to. And what's your name, little one?

Samantha.

Ah, . . . then you must be the Great Friedrich's little girl. He was telling me he had a will-o-the-wisp called Samantha.

Yes, he's my Dad. His real name is Henry.

Is it now?

Yes. He had to change it though – for his act.

And no wonder. Henry doesn't sound quite grand enough for a bear trainer, does it? Not to be compared with the Great Friedrich.

No. What's your name?

Me? I am Pochetto, the clown with the thousand pockets!

No, I mean your real name.

Oh, it's not much of a name either. Just plain Patrick.

It sounds all right to me.

Why, thank you indeed.

Are you going to play in the matinee?

Just about to make-up for it I was, when your little face appeared in my mirror. And what do you do, help your clever father with his bears?

No. He doesn't want me to work with the bears. He wants me to be like my mother was – the next Madame Miracle, he says.

I don't think I've met your mother yet. What act does she do?

She doesn't any more. She's dead.

Oh, sorry I am to hear that.

She used to dive through fire.

My! Did she now? And who'll be training you for tricks like that?

Renata. I don't like her though. I don't like her lessons. Sometimes, I think I don't like the circus much.

What's this you're saying? Come on, you must be liking the circus Samantha, with a father called 'The Great Friedrich'.

Would you call me Sam instead of Samantha? I don't like Samantha.

6

I think Samantha's a fine name, but if you're wanting Sam, then Sam it is. And what will you be calling me?

Um . . . Patrick. Because I met you first before you put your make-up on.

Then let's be shaking hands on it before my hands are covered in cream.

Your hands really shake. Are you nervous, Patrick?

I must be, mustn't I? Even though I've done my act many times before. But now for the 'smell of the greasepaint and the roar of the crowd' as they say.

Can I stay and watch a bit?

I suppose so, if you haven't anything else to do.

No, I haven't. Is that your trick coat over there?

Don't be fiddling with it now, if you don't mind. But say, if you know about my trick coat, then you must have seen my first performance last night?

Yes, I did.

And did it make you laugh, Sam?

Mm . . .

You don't sound too sure, girl.

Well, I laughed when water and all that yucky stuff came pouring out from the coat. Where do you hide it all?

Ah! That's a secret now. The secret of a Pochetto coat. All the Pochettos have worn coats like that one.

Were there other Pochettos before you?

Surely.

How do you know that?

Well, I can't prove it, mind, but I'm pretty sure of it.

7

Who was the very first?

Ah, let me see, that must have been Pochetto the Premier.

What does premier mean?

It means the first.

Then, he'd have to be called that if he was the first.

Yes, well, he was the one who discovered the coat.

How did he do that?

Oh, that's quite a long story, Sam.

I'd like to hear it.

Would you now? Wouldn't you be better off listening to stories of fire-divers and acrobats and people like that?

I'd rather hear about clowns.

Pochettos weren't always clowns, you know.

I'd still like to hear about them.

Mm . . . I was afraid you'd say that. Well, perhaps when I feel in the mood — when the visions of my famous forebears are clear in my not-too-clear head. That's when you shall hear about them.

What about after the matinee?

Oh, as soon as that, eh? A determined little lady, aren't you? I wouldn't like to be a bone if you were a dog. Here now, don't look so down-in-the-mouth. I suppose I could spare some time for the next Madame Miracle.

Please don't call me that.

All right Sam. You can come back here after the show. But you'd better be giving me some peace and quiet right now — I have to be ready in half an hour. Besides, your father might be wondering where you've got to.

No he won't. He's always too busy training his bears. He wouldn't care.

I'm sure he would, you know. Run along now Sam.

'Bye Patrick. Oh, good luck with the matinee. I'm so glad you've joined this circus.

Well, thank you fair lady — that has made my day.

THE POCHETTO COAT

'm here Patrick.

I see that.

Are you ready to tell me about the first Pochetto?

Just let me wash off this Pochetto first, and then we might be ready. They gave me only one chair for this little caravan, so if you don't mind, Sam, I'll rest my weary bones in it, while you sit on the floor, or if you like, on the doorstep there.

I'm sorry Patrick. Would you rather not tell me the story today?

No, no, Sam. A promise is a promise. I'll be right in a minute. It's just that I'm not as lively as I used to be. But as long as some folk still laugh out there, I suppose I'll keep going.

I heard a lot of people laughing at you.

That's good to know. Now, I'll just have a quick nip to wet the whistle, and then we'll start . . . Ah! That's better now.

What is that stuff?

It's my medicine — nothing like it to warm you up and loosen the old tongue.

Can I try some?

Oh, no. I wouldn't be feeding you this stuff, Sam. If you're wanting a drink, then I'm afraid it'll have to be water.

No, I don't really want a drink.

Wise girl! Now then, off we go. I think I said I'd tell you how the first Pochetto got his name, didn't I?

Yes, and about the coat too.

Well, it was all because of the coat . . . You see, there was once an actor, famous for playing nasty parts. Rollo, for that was his stage name, loved to dress up in the blackest of robes, wear the blackest of false beards, and the blackest of broad hats. He had a voice for every villain he played. He could sneer or shout, growl or snarl, whichever was needed. Though he was six feet four inches tall, he could sneak around on tip-toe just as easily as tramping like the giant he was. There were always people in the audience who felt like hissing him whenever he appeared, but even though they knew in their insides that it was only acting, they were afraid of him, and stood at the back, or kept low on their benches, just in case he might leap from the stage and glare at them nose to nose.

Though he was always cast for the bad parts, this Rollo wasn't such a bad fellow when he left the stage and hung up his costume — not like some I've known in my time, and they were supposed to be clowns too! But he was vain, oh yes Sam, he loved himself did our Mr Rollo. And he did have a bit of a temper too — just one button missing from a jacket was

11

enough to send him off. All the tailors bustled about to have everything just so for Rollo, but often they didn't please him.

It was during one of these missing-button scenes that a lively young fellow came to his dressing quarters.

'Come in, if you have me buttons, stay out if you haven't', shouted the great actor. His barking didn't scare this visitor away.

'Mr Rollo sir, I haven't brought your buttons, but I could look after your wigs and costumes better than any tailor. And if it's baggage, or learning lines, then I'm your fellow, and no mistake.'

Even Rollo was taken by surprise at this cheek. 'What is your name, bold midget?' he asked.

'Fellipe, sir!'

'Well Fellipe, you aren't trying to tell me you can read as well as sew, and you such a little whipper-snapper?'

Fellipe stood up as tall as his five feet would allow. 'That I can, and I am willing for you to test me out if you don't believe me. I am older than I appear. I am nearly eighteen summers old.'

Rollo eyed him up and down. 'Then you'll be needing food in case you start growing late, and who'll be providing you with that?' he demanded, pulling one of his stage faces.

'I thought you might give me one good meal a day in return for serving you, Mr Rollo. That is all I ask, apart from standing beside the stage to watch you act.'

'Aha, so you want to learn to act, my boy? Then wise you were to see me first', said the vain Mr Rollo.

It must have been Fellipe's flattery that decided the matter, because he was hired then and there for a trial, starting straight off by finding the missing buttons and sewing them back on to the costume.

Well, so quickly and efficiently did Fellipe do this and all the other things that Rollo asked of him, that it wasn't long before he won his master's favour. From then on, Rollo never travelled to any new playhouse without his costume boy. Even when the players played before kings at their courts, Fellipe would be there behind the scenes. It was only when Rollo was invited to dine after a successful performance that Fellipe was left out. He didn't mind because it gave him the chance to try out some of the things he had learnt while watching his master at work. He copied every wave of the hand, or nod of the head. He memorized every line he heard. He paraded before the looking-glass dressed in one of Rollo's costumes. Looked a bit funny he did, though, because a coat of his master's would become a flowing robe on him, a shirt for Rollo would be flapping around Fellipe's legs. He tried to look at himself as he practised Rollo's sword-play, or the famous mean look, the dagger-thrust, or the cunning glance. But good and all as he became with these, Fellipe knew he'd be having trouble with his size. Short of wearing stilts, there wasn't any way he could alter that, but just wait and hope that he might grow taller.

He hadn't grown much more, however, when he had his chance to play before a real live audience, not a make-believe one or a looking-glass. And this is how it happened, Sam.

Rollo had stayed out late celebrating his success in the latest play, playing the part of a cruel cousin to a handsome duke, he was. Everyone at the party kept asking the players to act out the most popular scene from the play. This was the scene where the duke and the cousin are having a furious sword-fight, and just as Rollo is about to stick his sword into the duke's heart, a sorcerer appears and casts a spell on the sword. In a twinkling its blade breaks in two, and then the pointy end just dangles down. Then Rollo had to cry out, fall to his knees and beg forgiveness of the duke he had hated so much. Oh, he did the act very well. The audience couldn't work out how the trick sword operated, and that is why the people at the party wanted the players to act the scene over and over again.

How did the trick sword work, Patrick?

Well you see Sam, at just the right moment, Rollo would pull a trigger concealed in the handle of the sword. By means of a black thread, this would release a tiny catch at a hinge half-way down the blade, and then down would drop the pointed half. Because he was waving it about, and because the audience was never too close, they couldn't see how it was done, not even those at the party after he had acted it three or four times.

Well, what with all the food and drink and the extra acting, he didn't feel very well the next day. Fellipe was always careful to try to please his master on days like this. His main job was to try to have him ready for the next performance. He would coax him to drink some warm milk or eat a dry oatcake or two, the only food that Rollo could stomach when he felt bad.

Came that afternoon, and Fellipe laid out the costumes. Were they in a mess! Oh yes! Spattered with food and wine they were, but the little fellow sponged them clean and sprinkled perfume over them to sweeten them up for Rollo to wear again. Then came the terrible business of getting his master on his feet and dressed. All on his own, Fellipe pushed and pulled to move the mountain lying on the couch. He tried sticking pins into it. He tickled it. But all he got for his trouble were kicks and moans from it. Never had Rollo been as bad as this.

When the other actors called in to see how Fellipe was getting on, he told them he'd have his master ready in time. But half an hour before the performance was due to commence, when the first customers were coming into the playhouse, Fellipe grew desperate. He fetched a large bucket of ice-cold water and sloshed the whole of it over him. Well! That brought the mountain to life it did. Rollo rolled off the couch, staggered to his feet and then lumbered about, trying to find Fellipe.

'I'll teach you to act rainmaker!' he roared.

Fellipe dropped the bucket and dived into the costume rack. After him came Rollo, tearing down shirts and coats. Fellipe saw to his dismay the carefully cleaned costume kicked and trampled under the heavy feet. He managed to avoid Rollo's grasping hand by darting away and sliding under the couch. Rollo tried to follow him, but the bucket was in the way, and down he tumbled, costume-stands, looking-glass and all. Fellipe heard Rollo's head hit something — bucket or floor, or even the looking-glass. Peering out from his hiding-place, he could see the toppled mountain lying quite still. Now it was safe to come out.

Was his master dead though? Poor Fellipe rushed to find out. Relieved he was to hear the big heart thumping along as strong as ever. But things were still bad enough — there would be no play for Rollo that afternoon. Fellipe couldn't lift him up, so he piled costumes around him where he lay to keep him warm. But now what to do? He knew that no other actor had learnt Rollo's words and actions except . . .

Himself!

That's right Sam. And Fellipe began to argue with himself about it. I could do it, he thought. I have followed every move. But what about my size? I can swordplay as well as Rollo, but oh dear, what about the costume all crumpled and torn on the floor?

Just then, he remembered the trunk where Rollo had said he kept all his old costumes from his past successes. Fellipe hadn't had a chance to explore in it before, but now was the time to open it up. It didn't take him long to unsnap the lock and lift the lid. He didn't much like the musty smell that rose up from the old costumes but this was no time to be fussy. Although he was in a hurry, he turned each costume over carefully until he uncovered a richly embroidered jacket. This will suit the part, he thought. Of course, like all of Rollo's costumes, it trailed on the floor when Fellipe wore it, but there was no time to alter that. He had his own tights, so if nothing else fitted, at least they did. The floppy velvet hat he chose kept dropping over his eyes. But he wasn't going out on that stage bareheaded. Besides, the hat made him look a little taller. Considering how quickly he put on his make-up, Fellipe was proud of his appearance, and with a wig and a curled moustache, he hoped the audience wouldn't notice that he was too young for the part.

All the time he was dressing, he kept repeating the lines he would have to speak. He tried to imitate Rollo's deep voice, but he quickly gave that up when he realized his voice came out like yodelling. Now, all he had to do was to strap the sword on, and he would be ready. My, but did he have trouble with that, Sam! The belt went nearly twice around his middle. He kept punching extra holes in the leather until the belt felt firm enough. When he finally buckled it on, he found that the sword was so long that the scabbard kept getting caught in his coat tails as he walked forward.

What's a scabbard?

It's the holder for the sword blade. You wouldn't want a sharp thing like that tickling your legs! So, there was nothing Fellipe could do about it except hold the sword handle all the time with the scabbard stuck out behind him like a long stiff tail. When the call came for him to go out on the stage, he shook a little, like me, but he bucked himself up by whispering his opening lines before striding out as tall and as steady as he could manage.

The audience expected Rollo to appear, and when little Fellipe came on, a few began to laugh, and one or two made rude cat-calls. This made Fellipe angry, so he delivered his opening speech as sneeringly as he could. He must have sounded convincing enough because the audience immediately hushed and settled down to follow the action. But though he spoke his lines well, Fellipe did look odd when he moved about. Fortunately, nothing really serious went wrong until the sword-fight scene.

'Now Duke, prepare to meet thy death', he cried. Gripping the handle of the sword even tighter, he tried to withdraw it from the scabbard, but it wouldn't budge. He decided to say the line again much to the duke's surprise.

'Now Duke, prepare to meet thy death!'

The duke waited, watching poor Fellipe trying to pull the sword from the wobbling scabbard. The actor playing the duke had trouble keeping a straight face. It was too much for some in the audience. They began to laugh again. In pulling and pulling, Fellipe tripped on the coat and tumbled to the floor. Even from down there he shouted, 'Now Duke, prepare to meet thy death!'

After this, the sorcerer too started to giggle. Fellipe somehow managed to get to his feet. He gave one more tremendous heave on the sword, and out it came. But with all this tugging, Fellipe must have pressed the secret trigger. He looked at the sword in horror as it dangled in front of the duke before the sorcerer had time to cast his famous spell. But even worse, Fellipe had slashed the lining of the old coat, and along his arm, then down the sword and out over the stage scampered a family of mice who had been nesting in the costume. They tickled him as they ran out, and he capered about shaking mice everywhere. The sorcerer and the duke were rolling on the stage floor with laughter. The mice fled into the audience. Screams, laughing, shouting from there too. Fellipe tried to escape from the stage in shame but his wretched coat tripped him up again and he fell in a heap.

The audience loved it. Forgotten was the evil cousin he should have been playing. They stamped and cheered for the comic cousin with the broken sword and the trailing coat full of mice. It was the end of Fellipe the great stage bad man, but the beginning of Fellipe the great stage funny man.

You see Sam, he was wise enough to realize that mistakes are sometimes lucky, if you know what to make of them. As soon as he could, he set about making himself a special costume. Yes, that was the beginning of the coat with the thousand pockets, and he gave himself the name Pochetto, which is just another way of saying 'pocket'. And while Pochetto the First may have hidden only mice in the pockets, others who took the name after him thought up all sorts of strange things to hide in the lining of their coats.

My Pochetto coat here is very precious to me, Sam. It gives me my name, and helps me to be a clown, and what more can you ask of an old old costume than that, eh?

What happened to Rollo?

Oh, he got over his fall, and then he was just as good as ever. And what a lucky play group it was. If a villain was wanted, they had the Great Rollo. And if a funny man was wanted, well, they had . . .

The Great Pochetto!

That's right. The Great Pochetto.

You are not called the Great Pochetto, are you Patrick?

No, no. Just plain Pochetto — that's about my billing. And now, I think it's about time for you to go for tea.

Can I come again and hear other Pochetto stories?

You know something Sam, I quite enjoyed the telling myself. So you'll be welcome you will. If I'm busy telling you stories, I mightn't be needing as much medicine now, might I?

I suppose not. 'Bye Patrick.

'Bye Sam.

THE JESTER

What's the matter with you today, Sam?
Oh, nothing.
It doesn't look like nothing.
It is, though.

Then smile a bit. Here, hand me that pile of plates and I'll cheer you up with my clumsy waiter act. Now, you see, I balance a plate of spaghetti here, a plate of stew here, and another here, and here, and here, and here, and lastly, a huge plate of angel food jelly on my head like this. Now, off I go in and out the tables like so . . . and so . . . and so . . . and so . . . until my brother clown, Feste, sticks out his cane and I trip like this! But I save this plate, and this, and this, and this, and this, but not . . . not the angel food!

No smiles? Oh well, I suppose without the food on the plates, it's a bit hard for you to imagine. Maybe it isn't very funny anyway.

Oh yes. I'm sure it would be, Patrick.

No, no, Sam, don't be polite. You're right. Just because I

think it's funny doesn't mean you have to think it is too. But you'd think after all my years of clowning, I ought to know what children like.

I like your stories.

Ah yes, but I don't go out in the ring to tell stories, do I?

No, but lots of people laugh when you are Pochetto.

So you keep telling me Sam. I just hope you're right.

Could I have another Pochetto story now?

Another Pochetto story? Wasn't one enough?

You said there were others.

You're not going to let me forget, are you Sam?

You said some of the other Pochettos weren't always clowns.

So I did.

What were they then?

Oh, jesters, musicians, you know, folk like that.

Could you tell me a story about a jester?

You want a jester story? Now what made you pick a jester?

Because I don't know what jesters were supposed to do.

Oh well, that's easy enough. They had to amuse kings and queens and dukes, people like that — cheer them up by doing funny acts. If you were a queen, I wouldn't have been much good as your jester today.

Did they wear a costume?

Mostly, yes. It was of two colours, like one leg red, one leg yellow; half a jacket red, the other half yellow. Their caps and shoes were coloured too, with bells on the points.

Did Pochetto the Jester wear those?

Yes, I'm sure he would, except that his costume was very old.

It had become tatty and frayed at the edges, and of course he wore the famous coat of many pockets. It was a bright red and yellow one like his jacket and tights.

Did he look like you?

Well now, I'm not sure about that, but I'm sure that my hair isn't as white as his was. His hair was long and wispy. So were his eyebrows. He had a long nose, a gappy grin, and ears that could wiggle both together or one at a time.

I can wiggle mine together.

So you can. We'll be turning you into a jester before long!

Did he do acts for children like you do?

Yes. He spent a lot of time with the children at the court when he wasn't needed for the king's amusement.

Did they laugh at him?

Oh surely. And that was the trouble really. Pochetto was about the only fun the king's son Paul ever had. I'm afraid Sam, that this story, like so many others about jesters, has some sad moments.

I don't mind.

Are you sure? You didn't look too cheerful when you first came in to see me.

Yes. I want a story like that today.

All right then. Well, you see, the prince's mother, the queen, had died, and after that the poor lad lost interest in most things. But old Pochetto could always cheer him up. He used to let Paul dress up and take parts in little plays they made up for the other children. Paul was very good with the acting. But I'm afraid his tutors didn't like him spending so much of his time on what they thought were foolish pastimes. They wanted him to concentrate more on learning to be a king, and actors and jesters just didn't make kings. Paul had to learn more serious things. But try as they might, they couldn't interest him in battles or foreign geography or whatever else kings needed to know. The tutors were worried, and so was the king when they told him. They blamed Pochetto, and although the king liked his old jester, he blamed him too. The king consulted his chancellor about it.

Was he important?

Who, the chancellor?

Yes.

Oh yes, very important he was. King's right-hand-man really.

'Sire', said the chancellor, who was one of the few people who didn't like Pochetto, 'why not banish your jester from the court for a time, and then the Prince might forget these foolish games they play together?'

'But that will not help the problem of finding things to interest my son, and besides, I don't like to treat my jester too harshly — he means well', said the king.

The chancellor thought for a moment. 'I think I have a plan which would kill two birds with the one stone. Let's ask Pochetto to search the kingdom for a worthwhile toy to interest the Prince, a toy to take the place of those acting games they play, something unusual and rare', he said, very pleased with himself.

'But think of all those things we have tried already', said one of the tutors, 'toys and games of every description. They interest the other children but not the Prince any more.'

'Then it will make Pochetto's search all the more difficult, won't it?' said the chancellor, smiling.

The king was so stuck for ideas that he agreed. 'Send him away then Chancellor, but make certain he takes enough money. I don't want my old fool wandering the streets of the kingdom like a beggar, though that coat of his makes him look like one, I must say. Besides, if by chance he does find a rare toy, then I want him to reward the craftsman who made it.'

When the chancellor told him about the idea, Pochetto wasn't a bit keen to go, but in those days, Sam, if a king commanded, then you did as you were told. But he did grumble.

'What am I supposed to look for? What about my old legs? How will they carry me all over the kingdom?'

Letting him sort through all the toys already given to Paul didn't help Pochetto much, but at least the king gave him a strong donkey to give his legs a rest now and then. No, there was no way out of it, so he set about preparing for the journey. He fitted a little jester's cap between the donkey's floppy ears.

Now, my donkey and I look more of a pair, he thought. Those bells will jingle, and advertise our arrival in each town. And I must rehearse an act to gather a crowd together, especially the children, because then I can ask them about makers of rare toys in their town. The sooner I find this rare toy, the sooner I shall be back in my proper position as court jester.

Paul was sad to see his old friend going. He and the other children made up a little play about it. The chancellor was the villain in it, of course!

It was just as well Pochetto took extra leather with him, Sam, because he found that his shoes were always wearing thin with all the tramping he had to do. Pretty rough going between each town it was, and he didn't feel like giving the donkey the extra load of his old body too often.

The further he travelled, the more towns he visited, the more downcast he became. Of course, being a jester, he didn't show it, but he felt it inside. Not that he didn't find any toymakers — there seemed to be at least one in every town he visited. No, it was just that they all were making things Pochetto had already seen in Paul's collection. He didn't dare take back something that wasn't rare and unusual. So, disappointed each time, he would thank the toymakers for bringing out their special treasures, and then set out for the next town.

One day, he topped a rise overlooking the sea, and weary though he was with months of travelling, he quickly felt refreshed when he looked down on a small town known as Baito. What a view it was, with the blue, blue sea, and the crisp white houses all jumbled about down the hillsides to the water's edge. The path Pochetto was following disappeared around the steep slopes, but looking down, Pochetto could pick out a busy square beside the boat harbour.

That's the place for my act, he thought, the place to find out about the toymakers of this fine little town.

26

Without waiting to rest, he started off down the stepped streets. Of course, he collected followers as he went. The jingling of the bells brought some to their windows to wave, and children hung about in doorways to watch the funny old stranger with the dressed-up donkey. Yes, by the time he reached the square, he knew he wouldn't have much trouble gathering an audience together. The square, you see, was used as a market-place. The fishermen and their womenfolk sold their catch straight from boats moored on one side of it. So crowded it was, that Pochetto had trouble finding a hitching-post. The donkey didn't like the crowd pressing around and the children anxious to make friends with him. But once he was tied up and a nose-bag slung around his neck, he always ignored everybody.

Although Pochetto had attracted some attention already, when he took out his pipe, sprang up on to the fountain in the middle of the square and capered along its edge, an audience quickly crowded round. Children at first, but then quite a number of the older ones put down their baskets and stood watching. They took to clapping in rhythm when he piped a familiar tune, and one or two of them sang as well. Pochetto felt he could now commence his pantomime.

He put away his pipe, and introduced himself as Pochetto, the king's one and only jester for twenty years; Pochetto, clown of a thousand pockets! His first routine was to peer down into one of his sleeves and pretend to beckon to whatever was inside to come out. One by one, twelve pure white doves fluttered out to fly up and wheel round and round the square. What a sight it was, and how the audience loved it, especially when Pochetto started flapping his floppy sleeves as though he wanted to fly after them, and overbalancing into the water up to his thighs.

'Ducks is not doves!' someone shouted out from the audience, and when Pochetto struggled out to flap again, the children called, 'Fly, Pochetto, fly!'

Climbing on to the centre pedestal of the fountain, Pochetto stretched his arms wide and called up, 'Come down, come down my little white clouds.'

The crowd couldn't believe it when they saw the doves fly down to rest six on each arm in a regular line. Pochetto made everybody laugh by lifting one leg and posing like a fountain statue. He and the doves remained as stiff as marble itself until he blew out from his mouth some water he had been saving. He looked just like a gargoyle.

Well, he went through trick after trick like this. One of the doves, a little one called Pi, kept diving into the pocket where some seed was hidden, and Pochetto would pretend he hadn't noticed until the children shouted, 'Pi is at the seed again', and then he would feel about in the pocket for a few moments before bringing Pi out to scold her with a lot of finger wagging. Then she would hide her head in her wing. Oh, the children did love that. He finished by shouting, 'Fly away my little clouds', and then each dove flew once around the square and returned to disappear into one of Pochetto's sleeves. The show was over.

Now, just like you, a number of the children wanted to

know the secrets of the Pochetto coat, and they crowded around him after the act. He agreed to show them some of the secrets if they in return would help him with his search. Some of them said they knew of toymakers in Baito, so he opened out his jacket, and there, heads poking out from twelve separate holes in the lining, were the doves.

Do you ever put live things in your Pochetto coat?
No Sam. You see, I'm not much of an animal trainer, so I stick to my tricks with water and things, but I'd like to be able to produce a flock of birds from the jacket, that I would. And talking of water, I'm feeling a bit dry — think I'll oil up the old throat . . . Ah! that's better.

What about the toymakers of Baito?
Well, it seemed as though it would be the same old story — more soldiers and dolls — until one lad standing at the back spoke up. 'Old Eric isn't exactly a toymaker, but he's the cleverest man in the world', he said.

A couple of the other children giggled at the boy for this, but Pochetto smiled at him and asked him to come forward.

'What's your name, young fellow?'

'Most people just call me Kip.'

'Well Kip m'boy, tell me a bit more about old Eric.'

'Eric has a house full of boats.'

The others laughed at this, so Kip quickly added, 'They're models, he was a great sailor you see. I know all about the models because once I helped him carry stuff home from the chandler's, and now he lets me do odd jobs for him, like sweeping up the shavings and running errands to the town.'

'And what's so special about the models?' asked Pochetto.

'If you saw them, you'd know. He told me some of them took years to build.'

'I like the sound of your Eric the boatmaker, Kip. Could you show me the way to his shop?'

Just then, Kip thought of something. He hung his head and kicked at the ground. Pochetto asked him again, 'You can take me to him, can't you Kip?'

The lad tried to put him off. 'Eric doesn't like visitors much. He lives all alone and . . .'

Pochetto knew what Kip was thinking. 'You won't have to come inside and I won't be telling old Eric that you showed me the way, how's that?' he said.

'I'll take you there then', said Kip, looking relieved.

So the other children drifted away, Pochetto unhitched his donkey, and Kip led the way along the seafront. It was a busy place, a street of chandlers and traders, innkeepers and fishermen, but it wasn't long before the paved street petered out into a couple of wheeltracks. The sea wall stopped, and a rough bit of beach stretched ahead of them. There was only a handful of fishermen now, working away at boat-hulls or mending their nets. Then the two tracks merged into one — nothing on the beach now except the odd rotting boat with the wind singing through its holes. Pochetto was just about to ask Kip how much further they were going, when the boy stopped and pointed across a bay to a shack perched alone on a headland.

'That's Eric's house out there', he said, without moving on.

'Then I'll leave you here and go on alone. You can mind my donkey if you like', said Pochetto.

Kip was pleased to be left and to hold the donkey. He held the halter firmly as he watched the old jester walk away towards the lonely house. He was hoping that Pochetto would keep his promise not to tell Eric who had brought him there.

As Pochetto came closer, he could see that Eric's house was nearly surrounded by water — ocean at the front, estuary on one side, and a slack lagoon at the back. Almost a miniature island, you might say. After knocking on the heavy front door, and while he stood waiting for an answer, Pochetto noticed the windows — not windows at all, Sam, but port-holes set high in the walls out of his reach. No good trying to peer inside to see if anyone was at home, so he knocked again and again. When the door finally opened, he had his next surprise — a great craggy head poked out just under the door lintel, high above him.

'And who might you be?' it asked.

'I am Pochetto, king's jester, and I am looking for Eric, who, I am told, is a maker of ship's models extraordinary.'

'And who told you you'd be findin' him here?' was the craggy head's reply. Pochetto didn't want to lie about who had shown him the way, so he said that many people in Baito knew about Eric and his models. The head came right out then.

'And I know it was that young ruffian Kip what brought you here, through me spy-hole I seen him and a stringy-lookin' animal of yours too — both of 'em a skulkin' down on the beach.'

Of course, Pochetto stood up for the lad. 'Young Kip didn't want you to be disturbed, but I made him bring me here. I have come to you in search of a toy, a toy so unusual that it might serve to awaken interest in my young Prince Paul, so his tutors say. One of your models may be just the thing to kindle a spark in him, so please help me, Eric.'

Eric just grunted. He didn't much care about a distant prince. Pochetto didn't give up, though. He used one argument after another, but it wasn't until he told Eric how far he had travelled, and how he had been banished from the court for doing nothing but entertain the prince, that you would have seen that Eric wasn't as gruff as he first appeared. Being an old sailor, he admired courage, and he saw that Pochetto had a ton of it.

'Beckon the lad up from the bay then', he finally said, 'and you can both come inside. Kip can be doin' a spell of tidyin', while you look over the vessels.'

Eric followed Pochetto to a spot where Kip could see them. Although the lad wouldn't have heard him, Eric shouted while Pochetto waved. 'Come on up you young traitor, and bring the old bag-o-wind with you.'

As soon as Pochetto stood inside the house, he knew why young Kip liked doing odd jobs for Eric. It was a place to set a young one dreaming — even looked like a ship's inside, it did, with beams stretched right across the room just above Eric's head. The portholes each had a platform with steps leading up. Pochetto could just see Kip standing at one of them, imagining his Armada sailing up the estuary. Standing at another, a lad might imagine galleys drawing closer to the beach, or from another, war canoes skimming across the lagoon.

But the models on stands all around the room, oh yes, they would set him dreaming too — galleons and men-o-war, lifeboats, rafts, and fishing boats. Large or small, they all carried a tiny wax or wooden crew, manning oars or winding capstans, a whole world of seafarers and their craft, all in this one snug room. And then there was the bench — melting pots and a forge, racks bristling with carving tools, and barrels of flotsam and jetsam from which Eric might fashion a bowsprit or a stern lantern. Oh yes, Sam, it was a place of dreams was old Eric's house, but mostly a place for doing. Why, it looked as though the old sailor lived out his whole life in this one room, even his bed and eating-table stood close to the forge.

Pochetto wandered about the room peering closely at each model, hoisting the sails on one, lifting the hatches of another. Any one of these could be a gift for Paul, he thought. What a choice to make! He came to a long Roman galley. A row of oars poked out from ports on either side. Squatting down, he could see part of the inside. Two rows of slaves manned the oars, and high up on the poop-deck stood the master of the vessel holding a long steering oar. But what intrigued Pochetto most was a large wooden key amidships. It must do something, he thought, but whatever it wound up, he couldn't see, no matter which hole he peeped through. It was not until

33

he had looked at all the models that he interrupted Eric to ask him about the galley. Eric said nothing, but put down his tools, took the galley from its stand, and beckoned Pochetto to follow him.

'We're goin' to the lagoon, Kip', he said as he reached a small door at the back of the room. 'You can come too, if you like, lad.'

Kip put away his broom and ran to a raft model. Eric turned to Pochetto as they went out. 'Always wantin' that one he is when we go down to the lagoon. Be playin' at shipwrecks all the time he would, if it weren't for the jobs I give him.'

Kip passed the two of them, ran down to the edge of the lagoon, held up his finger to test wind direction, and then moved quickly around to his favourite launching spot. His sail was set, and the tiny raft and its shipwrecked crew were afloat before Eric and Pochetto reached the edge of the water.

Without saying anything, Eric held the galley firmly with his fingers between the oars, and wound the key gently and deliberately ten times, counting aloud as he turned it. On the count of ten, he made an adjustment to the steering master, and then lowered the craft into the water, pointing it towards the opposite bank before letting it go. To Pochetto's amazement, the oars stroked through the water, pushing the galley forward. Five firm strokes it made, and at the end of the fifth stroke, the little steering master jerked from one side to the other, and the galley turned about. Five more strokes, and it returned, not more than a few paces from where they stood.

34

Imagine how Pochetto felt about this, Sam. In those days, mechanical toys were almost unheard of. Here indeed was the unusual toy he had been searching for. Relieved he was to find that Eric was willing to part with it for the pieces of silver Pochetto carried with him.

'Remember though', warned Eric, 'not to wind the key any more than sixteen turns. Eight strokes will take her a long way, so measure your pond before launchin', and don't be forgettin' to set the steering master the same number of points as half the turns o' the key, and then she'll go about just fine. She's a delicate one, this one.'

This all sounded a bit complicated to Pochetto, so he had a few practices with the galley while Eric coached him. All this time Kip played happily with his raft, launching and re-launching it, dropping supplies, shouting 'Land ahoy', 'Man overboard' and other calls of the sea. Even when Pochetto shouted his thanks to him, he only looked up for a second and waved. Pochetto hoped that Paul would be as interested in the galley as Kip was in his raft.

And it certainly seemed as if Pochetto had made the right choice, at least as far as the king, the tutors, and even the chancellor were concerned. They agreed it was a suitable toy for a prince. But Pochetto noticed that Paul had changed since he had last seen him — all the fun seemed to have been knocked out of him. Even his greeting to Pochetto was half-hearted. He looked at the model politely enough. Pochetto hoped he would show more interest when he and Paul tried it out on the lake in the palace garden, but unfortunately they didn't get the chance to play with it quietly together because the king insisted on a public demonstration of the wonder toy. And so workmen were ordered to clear the lilies and the weed from part of the beautiful lake, and seats for the audience were placed close to the edge.

All eyes were on Pochetto as he stood holding the galley not far from the prince. He wanted to be sure of success first time, so, with much ceremony, he wound the key just eight times, set the helmsman, and then carefully launched the craft. As he stepped back to give everyone a clear view, he was relieved to see it start well. Four strokes propelled it away from the edge. He was even more relieved to see, at the fourth stroke, the helmsman swing over and the galley turn about. Some of the people watching whispered, 'Amazing!' and 'Clever old Pochetto!'

The king was delighted, especially when the galley returned almost at their feet.

'What do you think of that, Paul? Soon you will operate it yourself. Master of your own galley, eh?'

Paul didn't answer his father, but everyone thought that this meant he was more interested in the model. Pochetto gave the key twelve turns this time, and when the galley cut across the lake, several of the audience counted the strokes before it turned again. The old showman built up the interest by demonstrating a third time, confidently winding the key sixteen times. It nearly reached the opposite bank before turning, but even so, it returned close to the starting point.

The chancellor was becoming impatient with Pochetto.

'When shall the Prince command the galley, Pochetto?' he demanded.

'Why I am sure he is ready now, aren't you my son?' said the king before Pochetto had a chance to answer.

'Pochetto, bring it closer, and show the Prince how to set its workings', ordered the chancellor.

'Sire, the maker told me its workings are very delicate', Pochetto warned the king.

The king was impatient too. 'Oh come now, Pochetto, you have demonstrated enough. Let the Prince be its commander now.'

Paul was pushed up from his seat, and before Pochetto finished explaining why the galley should be wound and set carefully, a tutor grabbed it and told Paul to wind the key. Poor Paul didn't think to hold the oars before he launched it, so of course they rowed feverishly back and forth in the air. Pochetto managed to show him this much before he re-wound it. Without setting the helmsman, the prince clumsily launched the craft. It moved away quite well, but it didn't return. It stopped somewhere near the centre of the lake, and quite a business it was then retrieving it, calling for servants willing to risk a wetting poking the galley with long poles. The prince was taken around to the opposite side, and a tutor grabbed the galley when it came within reach.

The audience didn't see just how roughly the model was set and launched from there. Once again it failed to turn, and as the prince was brought back to retrieve it, Pochetto went across and tried to persuade the tutor to let him show Paul the workings of the galley again, but he was brushed aside.

'The galley is the Prince's', shouted the tutor, 'he should be able to command it'.

Poor Pochetto stood by helplessly as the prince started winding and making a third clumsy adjustment to the helmsman, but what horrified him most was to see the key wound many more turns than the sixteen Eric had said was the very limit. A nasty grinding noise came from inside the galley, but it was dropped into the water again. Now it behaved more like a dying water-beetle than a Roman galley. The oars plied out of rhythm. The little helmsman rocked to and fro. The galley made no headway at all, simply spinning madly near the edge of the lake. Its convulsions soon died down. The audience looked embarrassed. Paul snatched it up, and before anyone could stop him, he threw it as far as he could into the lake, where it immediately capsized and sank from sight.

So upset was the king by this, that the chancellor ushered everyone away. Paul didn't seem to care about the loss of the galley, although he did feel guilty for Pochetto's sake. It was left for Pochetto to decide whether it was worth fishing for. All his efforts had been spent for this one wasted performance, and he felt like leaving it there. But he thought of Kip and Eric, and decided to return it to its rightful home. Naturally he was miserable, as only clowns and jesters can feel miserable. If only they had let me show it to Paul on his own, he kept thinking.

But his permanent banishment from the court was certain now. Before he left, he gave Paul his jester's costume. Not the

39

coat, mind you, but the cap and bells, the jacket and tights. It was a sad parting for them both, even worse for Paul than for Pochetto because the old jester had found a place where he would be happy to spend his last days, where he would be welcome, and where, if he felt like it, he could perform one of his acts in the square.

At Baito?

Yes Sam, and of course he was always welcome at Eric's porthole house, or walking with Kip and the donkey along the seafront. No, Pochetto was happy enough, but for Paul, life as a prince, and later on as a king, was only brightened a bit by his love for dressing up and making plays for his own and his courtiers' amusement. It was the only way he could escape from everyone prodding him, and advising him, as they did that day with the Roman galley.

That's a sad story.

Well, I warned you, didn't I?

Renata prods me a lot.

I suppose she wants to make a good fire-diver out of you.

I'd rather do acts like you, Patrick.

And so you shall, girl — in between your other practices.

No, I mean I'd rather be a clown, not a fire-diver.

Oh, well now, I can't see your father or Renata agreeing to that — pretty rare it must be for a girl to turn to clowning.

You could talk to him, though.

Yes, I suppose I could, not that anybody takes much notice of me around here. But wouldn't it be better if I tried you out with a few things first to see if you are really keen about it?

Yes, but you'll find I am.

Well, we'll see about that. Next time you pay me a visit, I might have something ready for you.

Oh, good.

No promises mind. Now, off you go.

Thanks for the story, Patrick.

Mm, perhaps I shouldn't have told you that one today . . .
'Bye, Sam.

'Bye Patrick.

THE DREAM

Patrick! Patrick! Are you there?

What? Who's that? Who's that? Oh, it's you Sam. I must have been dreaming. Why, it's all dressed up you are, girl!

Yes. I'm trying some funny clothes. Do you like them?

Not going to give up, are you? But you look fine, your make-up is just fine, especially that old hat.

I could be a clown in these, couldn't I, Patrick?

Well Sam, you can start with the costume and the make-up, but then there's juggling and tumbling, and after all that, there are your acts, they have to come from somewhere.

Did you copy another Pochetto first?

Other clowns, yes, but that wasn't enough you know. Probably right for a clown to do that when he's learning, but there's a time when he has to think up routines for himself.

What if he can't think of any?

Then that's a sign he's not meant for clowning.

How do you think of things to do?

Sometimes I do just what I was doing when you called out.

But you were sleeping.

Not just sleeping. I was dreaming.

How does dreaming help you think of things?

It helps me to turn things upside down.

Eh?

Not really upside down, but I lie down, and before I close my eyes, I think of something, anything like, like say, a cup of tea or, or a circus tent even. Then, as I doze off, I think of that cup of tea or that circus tent in a place you wouldn't expect to find them — for instance in my shoe, or . . .

Or in the Pochetto coat?

Yes. Yes Sam, that's right, perhaps inside the coat. Then, as I dream off, my thoughts might get more mixed-up, with the tea-cup or the tent getting into all sorts of funny situations. And then, when I wake up, if I think the topsy-turvy troubles have been funny enough, I might use some of them in my acts.

Does your medicine help you to do it?

Why? Oh, you mean because I've been nursing this bottle? Yes, it does sometimes, but it can make dreams that are just mixed-up, not very funny at all. Pretty bad, those dreams can be.

What sort were you having just now?

Well, I'm rather glad you woke me up.

They must have been bad ones then 'cos you looked a bit funny when you saw me.

The dream wasn't all that funny.

43

What was it about?

It was about that circus tent.

What happened to it?

Nothing to the tent really, it was just stuck out in the middle of nowhere.

What was it doing there?

I don't know, I don't know.

Was there a circus in it?

I can see I won't get any peace until I tell you the rest of it. But it's not very nice, Sam.

I don't mind. I'm happy today in my clown clothes.

Just as well . . . I remember standing looking at this bump away in the distance. It wasn't until I walked near to it that I saw it was a circus tent, all on its own, no flags, no crowds of people queueing outside. I can't remember the number of times I walked round and round it looking for an opening. I could hear music from inside. Not the usual brass band, more a tinkling and a twittering sound. Then came a noise like the slashing of canvas. I saw what looked like a knife cutting a doorway in the tent from the inside. The canvas flopped down, and out stepped a lion dressed as a ring-master. He had used his long sharp claw to cut the tent.

'Step right in', he growled at me, almost pulling me through the opening.

Bright lights shone on the ring where a high wire was strung up. The band making the music was on one side — birds on perches were the musicians. There seemed to be dozens of them all twittering or shaking little cymbals and bells. I was pushed by the lion up to a high seat. Too dark it was to see who was seated around me, but I could hear peanuts being chewed, or that's what it sounded like. The lion bounded down into the ring, cracking his tail like a ring-master's whip. The band stopped.

He roared, 'I give you the Daring Dromedaries!'

And marching in came a family of camels all dressed in tights. It was a mystery where they came from because the only opening in the tent was the slash the lion had made. The camels bowed, and waved up to me.

I started to laugh when they balanced upside-down with their humps on the wire and their legs in the air. Something beside me growled to be quiet so I stopped. Those camels were as good as Renata, Sam, balancing on one leg, tossing rings to each other and catching them with their necks or their humps. They did all the tricks you would want to see, and when they finished by balancing one on top of the other, I clapped as hard as I could. But I couldn't hear anyone else clapping with me. The lights came up on the audience, and all the seats were empty except the one next to me. There, a great fat bear sat holding his bag of peanuts and his can of drink.

'What are you doing that for?' he growled at me, just as he had done before.

'I am clapping the camels', I replied.

'Well we don't like that sort of noise here, do we ring-master?'

'No!' answered the lion.

And with that, the bear pushed me off the bench and I

tumbled over and over the rows of seats down to the edge of the ring. They laughed, camels and all.

The lion said, 'Doesn't he tumble well? We might be able to train this one.' He came across and patted me on the head with his paw, gave me a sugar lump, and shoved me into the front row.

'And now, I give you Pochetto and the Twenty Dwarfs!' he announced.

'But that's me!' I shouted, jumping to my feet.

'Sit down in front', growled the bear, and he showered me with peanuts and peanut shells.

'Yes, down you sit', roared the lion, cracking his tail within an inch of my nose. So I sat down and watched.

His Pochetto was a floppy seal. He wore the Pochetto coat right enough. He started by rolling and gambolling head over tail as seals do. Then he fetched a stack of buckets which he tried to carry on his head or by his tail — juggling tricks like that. After a lot of fooling, he set them out in a circle with one upturned in the centre and, with a huge hose-pipe, he filled them all with water, wetting everything around. He sat down on the upturned bucket and called out, 'Where are my little fishermen?'

He undid his coat, and twenty little people jumped out and marched round him. Each was dressed as a clown. Each carried a net or a fishing rod over his shoulder. 'Left right, left right', cried the Pochetto seal. Then, when they were each beside a bucket, 'Halt!'

'Rods and nets ready?'

They nodded.

'Number one — fish!'

And the first of the dwarfs cast a line into his bucket. He hooked a fish bigger than himself which he tossed back to the seal. It disappeared down the seal's gaping mouth. Each dwarf in turn did the same with rod or net. The seal swallowed twenty fish one after the other. Just imagine, twenty fish at a time. Then the dwarfs all turned, marched round and round and back into the coat again. The horrible Pochetto seal bowed, and waved his flippers. I didn't feel like clapping this time.

The lion ring-master came over. 'So you didn't like that?' he roared. 'Then we shall see if you can do any better.'

The seal took my seat, surrounded by the camels, and I was dragged into the ring by one ear. The lion picked up a bucket and tossed it high above the ring. Then he picked up another, and another. Pretty soon he was juggling five. He finished by catching them one after another on his head. He took them off and placed them in front of me.

'Now then, my tumbling friend, it's your turn', he said.

I threw the first bucket up, but it hit the high wire and landed out of reach. The lion's tail-whip cracked near my nose again. I tried and tried. The whip kept cracking. I managed to juggle two. I was thrown another sugar lump. I failed to juggle three at first. The whip cracked again. I managed three. More sugar, cracking whips and sugar lumps. I was throwing four, five, six. Buckets going up and up.

'More!' they all roared, 'More!'

47

Buckets and buckets spinning up into the lights. And there Sam, was where you came to my rescue by waking me up.

I don't think I'll try dreaming for funny acts, then.

Oh, the dreams don't have to be like that one, Sam. And anyway, you can try the mixed-up idea without going off to sleep.

Can I try one now?

Well yes, I suppose you could. What can we think of to start you off?

You said this hat was funny already.

Yes. Yes, it is that. Now, think of that hat in a place it shouldn't be.

Mm, on my foot?

Yes, that's one. Anywhere else?

Um, I can't think.

What about eating out of it?

Eating out of it?

Yes, or drinking out of it? Let's say you eat a whole meal out of it.

I would have to do magic for that.

Yes, but that's not too hard if you practise. Just imagine now, an act where you come in and sit at a table in a cafe. Let's think about using that hat for everything. First, it's a bell and you ring it with a spoon to bring the waiter.

But it wouldn't make a bell noise.

Ah, right! So if you use this hat for clowning, you will have to alter it — hide something under the lining to make it ring, and lots of other things like that.

What a lot of trouble!

Well that, my girl, is what clowning is all about — a lot of preparation and practice, for just a few, few minutes of acting.

That's what Renata always says about fire-diving.

Yes, they all take practice, they all take practice, whether they are funny acts or daring acts, slow acts or fast acts. Are you sure you still want to be a clown?

Yes, I think so.

Then let's finish this imagining game about the hat. You try and help me now. The waiter comes in and hands you the menu. You can't read it because the writing's too small. You pick up the hat and use it like a magnifying glass to peer through. So the top of the hat would need a hole cut in it, wouldn't it? Now, imagine you can't hear what the waiter suggests. What do you do with the hat this time?

Mm, put it up to my ear?

That's it Sam, like an ear trumpet. Now you're getting it.

And the waiter shouts into it.

Good, good Sam, that's the idea. That's how clowns have to think.

THE SAPORENE TREE

hat's good Sam! Now try juggling two oranges. Leave your hands well apart, and throw in the same way as you did with one. Are you ready? *Yes.*

Off you go. Throw, throw, throw. Your hands are getting closer together. Keep them apart, Sam. Keep them apart! Oops! There. Never mind, try again. Throw one. Now two again, throw, throw, throw, throw. Good, that's four . . . five . . . six . . . Ah! there you go again. Have a rest now.

Could you show me what I am doing wrong?

Hand me the oranges, and I'll show you.

How can you juggle when your hands shake?

Oh, they don't shake all the time, Sam. And if I concentrate hard, I can still juggle — perhaps not as well as a few years ago.

Anyway, it doesn't matter if you drop things because that makes people laugh, doesn't it?

Ah yes, but there's a lot of difference between doing it by accident, and doing it on purpose, Sam. Watch! One orange

51

up, two oranges up. Up, up, up, up, and then . . . I drop one like this. See, you didn't laugh at that, did you? Now let's do it a different way. One orange up. Two oranges. Up, up, up, and then . . . one in the sleeve, and the other down my pants! You see, you smiled that time, didn't you?

Yes, but I didn't laugh.

I'll make you laugh. I sit down and I pull a face as though the orange in my pants is squashed in there. There! Now I get up and walk about as though the juice is running down my leg. See, you're starting to giggle, aren't you Sam?

Yes . . . Patrick?

Yes?

What happens if you do an act, and nobody laughs?

Oh, then you pay an army of small boys to crawl under the seats to tickle everyone with feathers.

You don't really, do you?

No, no. I was just kidding. The answer, young lady, is to give up. You can't make people laugh if they don't want to. Of course, it's mostly the clown's fault if they don't.

You are frightened that people won't laugh at you, aren't you?

Yes. Yes Sam, I am, that's true. A Pochetto like me has to be funny or he loses his job.

Have you a story about one who wasn't funny?

Aha, so we come back to stories again, do we? What about more juggling practice?

Could we have a story, if I juggle the oranges ten times?

Oh, I wouldn't be making you do that for a story, Sam. You just have a little practice there with the oranges, while I try to

52

remember a story about a Pochetto who lost his laughter.

Does that mean he couldn't laugh himself?

Yes, yes I suppose it would mean that. When an audience doesn't laugh at a clown, then a clown won't find much to laugh at, either. Now let me think.

Does your medicine help you to think?

I'm just opening this bottle to have ready in case my voice needs oiling. You concentrate on the oranges, lass — don't worry about me . . . Ah yes, I think I have the story for you — just pop those oranges back, and sit yourself down.

Well, this Pochetto thought he had lost touch with his audience, Sam. Once, he had been the star clown in the show, with an act of his own, but now he had to be content to run and tumble with the crowd of clowns who filled in between acts. He thought he must be sick. He filled his quarters with potions and powders. Tried every tonic and medicine he could find, he did.

Did he try your medicine, Patrick?

He did that, but it didn't do him much good either. He took to moping on his bed for hours instead of practising his tricks. One time, as the show was travelling from one town to another, Pochetto found himself riding beside Martha, the owner of this show. Great with animals she was — everyone came to her when their animals were sick or injured, or even just bad-tempered. No vets then, Sam. Some said she had magical powers, but this may have been said because she was also a fortune-teller.

She caught Pochetto swallowing some potion or other as

they jogged along. Martha didn't like to see her favourite clown miserable like this. Though she was very gentle with animals, she didn't have much time for weak humans.

'And what are you taking that stuff for, Pochetto?' she asked.

'Because I'm sick.'

'You don't look sick to me.'

'But I am. And I can't make people laugh because of it.'

'It's more likely the other way round', she said.

Pochetto thought about this for a moment. 'Would you have a brew to brighten me up, then?' he asked. 'Something that worked for the animals even.'

'Don't be silly Pochetto, it's not medicines I use on the animals — just herbs, and a lot of love. What you need to find is an audience who still think your act is funny, and then you'll feel better, as if by magic.'

'Where will I find an audience like that? All the towns we have played in this year have been the same for me. Not much interest in my clowning. And anyway, how can I tell if it's me they are laughing at, if all I do is a bit of tumbling with the other clowns?' Pochetto went back to sipping from his bottle.

'Have you ever played in the village of Saporene?' Martha asked.

'No.'

'Then we shall have to pay the Saporenes a visit when we tour the northern parts of the country.'

'What's so special about Saporene?' asked Pochetto, showing a bit of interest.

'Everyone, just everyone from the oldest to the youngest, is happy there.'

'Oh, I can't believe that, how could that be?' he said.

'You wait and see. If we make our visit at their festival time, then you should see what I mean. But you must make a special effort to prepare an act of your own to perform.'

Pochetto must have needed this bossing from Martha because, for the rest of the tour, he spent many hours at practice again. This was good because he didn't have as much time to swallow his potions or to mope on the bed. By the time they came to Saporene his act was ready.

Was everyone happy there, really?

Well it certainly looked that way to Pochetto, Sam. As they passed the cottages, he saw that all the window-boxes were bright with autumn flowers, and on the ledges inside, piles of fruit and produce had been arranged to make a fine show for anyone like Pochetto who cared to look in. The people's smiles and greetings to the players were as bright as the flowers.

When they came to the village square, Pochetto stopped his cart to gaze at a wonderful tree growing on the green. It was laden with fruit, remarkable fruit it was, about the size and shape of apples but with the skin divided exactly in half, one half golden yellow, the other half cherry red. Because the line between the two halves was so sharp, Pochetto thought at first that the fruit must be some sort of festival decoration, but when he got down from the cart and went up close to the tree, he could see that the fruit was actually growing on it. With a few autumn leaves still hanging from the branches, the tree made a rare sight, it did.

'That's the tree from which Saporene gets its name', said Martha, as Pochetto hopped back in the cart.

'I have never seen a tree like it.'

'And you won't anywhere else. I am told that they are only found in this valley. The villagers say that this one is the biggest and the best. It's their festival tree. We will make time to come down to the ceremony here before our show starts.'

Later that day, a bell was rung to call the people to the square, and the players, who had finished their preparations, joined the villagers around the Saporene tree. Then the mayor pushed his way through and addressed the people.

'My dear friends, and welcome visitors, now is the most important moment of the year for our village, when the Saporene tree gives us its fruit for our happiness and goodwill. So says the legend, handed down from generation to generation. I now call on Father Ambrose to bless our beloved tree.'

The village priest stepped forward, and after prayers, he sprinkled holy water on the Saporene tree from four different directions. Then he picked off a perfect fruit and gave it to the mayor. The mayor took over again.

'Thank you, Father Ambrose. And now, as is our custom, I will show the way, by taking the first bites.'

Saying this, he took a huge bite from the yellow half of the fruit. Oh, it must have tasted ever so bitter because the mayor's face puckered up as he struggled to chew the pieces. Everyone pointed and laughed at the faces he pulled. Pochetto wasn't sure if it was polite for visitors to laugh too, but when he saw that it was part of the ceremony, he joined in.

The mayor managed to chew his way through the yellow half, and then, with a look of relief, he took a bite from the red half. His expression changed as if by magic. It was obvious to Pochetto that this half must have been so delicious, that just the first mouthful brought a look of sheer delight to the mayor's face. The people clapped until he had swallowed the last sweet morsel and then they all cheered.

'Now, my friends', announced the mayor, smiling, 'I am assured of a happy year until we meet again, just one year from today around the Saporene tree. Gone is the bitterness of the old, and come is the sweetness of the new!'

With this ceremony, he stepped down, and each of the villagers followed the same ritual in turn. Quite a pile of cores was buried at the foot of the tree when everyone had finished.

Did Pochetto try eating one, too?

Oh yes. Visitors were always invited to become part of the legend. The children laughed as he tried to swallow the bitter half. Oh, it tasted revolting, he thought, but when he bit into the red half, he realized at once why such a change had come over the mayor's face. No other fruit had ever tasted as delicious as this, and more so after eating the bitter half.

How strange, thought Pochetto, that this is the secret of their happiness. But the test for him and his audience would come when he performed his act.

Late in the afternoon the show began, and soon after Pochetto first appeared, laughter broke out. Just to see

Pochetto staggering in with his bag of tricks was enough to set this audience off. He could hardly believe it. Of course, he played up to them, catching his nose in the legs of the folding table as he jerked it open, and collapsing the table two or three times; you know Sam, things like that. All this laughter so early in the act encouraged him, just as Martha had said it would, and he made up his mind to give them his best.

'Friends!' he shouted, pulling a wizard's hat from his bag, 'I am about to demonstrate my gifts — not just as Pochetto clown of a thousand pockets — but as Pochetto, wizard and sorcerer extraordinary!'

With a flourish, he donned the hat, and arranged on the table a collection that looked like his tonic bottles and medicine-flasks, and from one of his pockets he brought out the tiniest white mouse you ever saw.

'May I present my little friend Tiny', he announced, gently releasing him on to the table. Most of the audience had to strain to see the mouse as it darted about sniffing at the bottles and poking in the flasks.

'Can't you see him?' Pochetto asked the audience.

'No!' they shouted back.

'Then I shall have to make some growing tonic for him.'

Pochetto pretended to mix up all sorts of medicines. He sniffed the mixture, and then made a few passes over it.

'Abracadabra, ready, set, go,
    Make mouse bigger from top to toe.'

He held Tiny over the mixture for a moment, then popped him back under the Pochetto coat.

'One two three, four five six seven,

·My mouse has grown, or gone to heaven.'

He thrust his hand under the coat and brought out — not a large mouse, but a white rabbit.

'Oh dear', he wailed, 'I didn't want a rabbit, and where has my Tiny gone? But my secret mixture will magic him back.'

'Abracadabra, all round the house,

Change this rabbit back to a mouse.'

But each time that Pochetto tried to bring Tiny back, he produced something else from his coat by mistake — a white dog, a white cat, a white dove. He even arranged for a white horse to gallop on. The more mistakes he made, the more the audience laughed. In mock anger, he threw his bottles at the audience. Everyone·expected them to be solid but they were only made of paper and they burst as people tried to ward them off, showering them with, well, only water.

Pochetto chased the animals, tripping over his coat as Pochettos always do. He couldn't catch them so he stood still, took off the wizard's hat and blew it like a trumpet. Made a terrible blast it did, but the noise brought the animals back to stand by him, or perch on his shoulder, or jump up into his arms, all except Tiny mouse. He was nowhere to be found. Pochetto blew the hat again — the worst note of all this time. It trailed off into a gurgle, from a gurgle to a cough, from a cough to a choke. He looked down into the hat for the trouble, and what do you think he brought out of it?

His tiny mouse.

Right Sam. And that was how he finished his act. Oh, the

laughter and the clapping were music to Pochetto's ears, and he was to hear laughter like that many times again that year, not just in Saporene, but wherever Martha's show was playing. The only medicine flasks he needed now were the paper ones for his act. How pleased Martha was to see her favourite clown back in form again, and every year she was only too willing to let him return to Saporene for the festival, where he joined the villagers in the ceremony of the Saporene tree.

Why did the fruit make people happy, Patrick?

Well now, Sam, I don't think I have an answer for that, except to say that when people believe something very strongly, then it helps it to happen, and the Saporenes really believed in that tree and its fruit. Whether they would have been just as happy without it, I'm not able to guess. As for Pochetto, it was probably just as Martha said — all he needed was one good performance and then he could stop feeling sorry for himself. But who knows, it may have been because he had his Saporene fruit once a year!

And now, talking of fruit, how about one or two more throws with those oranges before you go off? Remember, Sam, you'll need lots of practice before you can make those mistakes on purpose. Are you ready?

Yes.

Right. Off you go. Throw one, throw two. Good, throw, throw, throw. That's fine! Five, six, seven, eight, nine, ten. Hooray! You made it!

See, I really am keen, aren't I, Patrick?

Yes Sam, I can see you are.

EPILOGUE: THE SWAP

Come on Sam, dry those eyes.

I don't want you to go, Patrick.

I know that.

I hate Renata.

No, no; don't be like that.

She said some horrible things about you. I don't believe any of them.

Some of them might be true, you know.

Well I haven't seen you drunk.

Maybe not for you, lass — just one or two doses of medicine to keep the stories coming, eh? Without you Sam, I might have had to leave the show even before this.

But you haven't been with it for very long.

It probably doesn't seem long to you, but it's been one whole tour — that's much longer than some other shows I've been with.

Renata said you weren't a good clown any more. That's not true. And she laughed when I told her you were teaching me. And Dad laughed too. And I said they were horrible, and that you were a good clown. Not the Great Pochetto, but a good one. And anyway, the Pochettos went right back to when there were kings and things, and you knew all about it because you told me stories about them. And some of them could do tricks and magic with the coat better than Dad ever does with his bears. That's true, isn't it Patrick?

Oh Sam, what have I done?

Don't you cry too, Patrick. It looks awful when grown-ups cry.

Pass me that bottle please, Sam. A quick dose of the old medicine might stop me. There! You see, I'm right again.

You don't look right.

No, maybe not, but there's something I have to do. Turn your back a minute, and promise not to peep until I say. Promise?

I promise.

Now . . . there!

But it's your coat! It's your Pochetto coat!

Yes, it's yours, Sam.

But what will you do without it?

Oh, I don't think I'll be needing it where I'm going.

Where will you go?

I think I'll be joining my old friend Mario the Magnificent.

Who's he?

Who is Mario the Magnificent, you ask? A great magician he is. Well, he was. He could make a whole family disappear with one flick of his fingers. He could bring them back with barely a whistle. Proud I was to be on the same bill with him — he with his great box of tricks, and me with my Pochetto coat.

Where does he live now?

Oh, just in a small house close to the city — but big enough for the two of us, plus his animals.

Would I be allowed to visit you there?

Well, I'd certainly be pleased to see you if you came, little one. You'd like Mario — he'd have some tricks to show you.

Has he kept his magic boxes?

Not the boxes, no. But he can still manage quite a lot of other tricks. He handed the boxes on to his apprentice, just as I'm doing with the Pochetto coat.

I'll bet his apprentice wasn't a girl.

What difference does that make?

The coat might fit me better if I was a boy.

Oh come now; fitting doesn't matter much does it? Remember Fellipe — tripping over the long coat helped him to be funny, didn't it?

But you're going away before I've learnt all about clowning.

Just keep on with the games, girl, and the rest will come soon enough.

Dad might stop me.

Hey, hey, all these excuses — you're not sounding much like my Pochetto apprentice. Nobody can stop you dressing-up and dreaming, can they?

No.

Right, so you start with the costume which is yours now, and you follow up with the dreaming, especially the funny mixed-up kind.

You don't think Renata would take the Pochetto coat away from me, do you Patrick?

No Sam, no. She's not so bad really. She might want you to clean it up a bit, but she wouldn't take it away from you. Now, why the long face still?

You won't be here to tell me any more Pochetto stories.

So that's it. Just think, Sam, I might have run out of Pochetto stories before long.

Aren't there any more?

Oh, perhaps one or two.

Couldn't we have one now? Just a small one.

Right now?

Please.

Oh well, what's the harm? One for the road as they say. We've had Pochetto the actor, the jester, the clown, and . . . how about Pochetto, the maker of a thousand sounds?

Sounds?

Yes. I'll tell you about the musical Pochetto. You see, he was a wandering minstrel, a one-man band. But he had a problem about the music he made, Sam — it was all just a bit too soft. He didn't like shouting or banging drums or clashing cymbals, so he soon discovered there wasn't a place for him in the circus or at fairs. He took to the streets instead, seeking out quiet corners to set up his stand. If he had been a barker, he would have introduced himself as 'Pochetto, player of a thousand instruments! Pochetto, maker of a thousand sounds!'

He didn't really have a thousand instruments though, did he?
Oh no, but his Pochetto coat was stuffed with all sorts of
funny pipes and gadgets, not only instruments that made
music, but some that made bird-calls, mouse-squeaks, or
even monkey-chatters. He could play many at one time, using
things like foot-bellows and mechanical strikers. Yes, he
really was a one-man band.

Only Doola, his little fox-terrier, shared the act with him.
Doola took round the hat while walking on his hind legs.
Without him, Pochetto wouldn't have made a living at all
because in most of the spots he played, people passing by
could only hear snatches of what he was playing, what with
the street noises and all. In their hurry, some would nearly
pass before noticing him. It was Doola's begging act that
persuaded them to stop and throw a coin into the hat. But few
people stopped long enough or stood close enough to hear the
haunting melodies Pochetto could play, or the quaint sounds
he could invent. Often, the street noises were so strong that he
couldn't hear the music himself. He always looked for quieter
places to practise, like under the bridges by the river.

But on this day, he found a new quiet place. Doola chased
after a cat, and Pochetto followed him up a narrow lane. It led
to a small square, surrounded by houses. In the centre of a
patch of grass grew a graceful tree with a bench encircling it.
Everything was peaceful and quiet. Pochetto decided to stay a
while and try out new songs and sounds, and perhaps polish
up a few of the old. When he started to play, his sounds were
trapped and held inside the square. He felt as though he was in

a theatre. Apart from Pochetto himself, only those who lived in the houses would hear the music he made, especially if they had left a window open.

Only one window was open that day and that was Connie's. Hers was often open. Connie wasn't much older than you Sam, but she'd never had the use of her legs and it must have seemed a lifetime to her that she had been kept in a chair, never able to move far without someone wheeling her, never able to run across that grass down there like little Doola. From where she sat, her view of the world was the square and the few people coming and going from it. She could see down the lane to the busy main street, but what a small part of the wide world that was! She watched Pochetto from the time he followed Doola into the lane.

Although he looked up and saw the open window with the lass sitting there, Pochetto didn't shout a greeting right away, in case she may have thought him rude and closed the window. He thought she was working at something with her hands, and he was right.

She may not have been able to walk but she certainly made good use of her hands. Her mother always made sure she had paper and pens, paints and brushes. She had drawn the square many times over — in the morning light with a touch of frost on the grass, in the brightness of sunlight when shadows were sharp, and in the softness of evening when the first lights appeared in the windows. But mostly she had drawn the world beyond the alley-way as she imagined it to be from things she'd read or from stories she'd been told.

But my, how quickly she drew while Pochetto was down in the square. Her pens scratched away at the paper at a furious rate. She drew him sitting there in his floppy coat, his instruments strapped on to his body, and his curly wire stand for his musical gadgets beside him. She put Doola in the picture too, holding the hat and begging, because although it was only a practice session, the little dog went through his routines just as if there were people all round them.

She only stopped drawing when she wanted to listen. Then, she shut her eyes, and the sounds took her away from the square — to the south seas and into the jungles, flying with a flock of birds or even chasing about in a mansion full of mice. One minute the music would bounce along, and the next it would float away into nothing.

She went back to her drawing when Pochetto stopped playing to take a break and have a bite to eat. From where she sat, Connie thought he was pulling out two more instruments, until she saw that one was a bread-stick and the other a long thin sausage. When her lunch came, it gave her the chance to ask her mother to go out and see if the musician had a name. You see, Connie was putting a border around her drawing, and she wanted to print the musician's name in it, in large bright letters. She watched her mother go across to him, and although she couldn't hear what they were saying, she knew when Pochetto smiled and waved, that her mother had told him why she sat at the window drawing.

Connie found she had just enough space to print 'Pochetto and Doola', although the 'and Doola' was in small letters. And

working hard, she had just enough time to finish the drawing and roll it up before Pochetto left the square.

He saw the roll of paper drop from the window and he came across to pick it up. He carefully unrolled it and looked at it admiringly.

'Connie, are you giving me this wonderful gift?' he asked.

She nodded shyly, a little surprised to find he knew her name.

'Then I shall give you something in return.'

Pochetto felt in the pockets of his coat and pulled out what looked like another bread-stick, and threw it up to her. She caught it easily. It was no bread-stick, but a pipe, hand-carved from hollow wood.

'See if you can get some sweet sounds out of that', he said.

'But . . .' Connie started to protest.

'No buts, mind — just cover the holes with those clever fingers of yours, and blow gently.' And before she had time to protest any more, he was off down the lane.

Did she learn to play it?

Oh yes, and she did make some sweet sounds after a little while. But the pipe, precious though it was to her, and even though she played it every day, never took the place of her drawing.

And did Pochetto come back to hear her?

No Sam, only once did he come to that particular square. His minstrel wanderings took him on to other places. But once was enough, for every time that Connie played the pipe, she heard not only her own notes but all the notes and sounds that

Pochetto had made that day, sounds that never failed to carry her away from the square, sounds that turned into pictures for her clever hands to draw.

And one visit was enough for Pochetto, too. Now he had Connie's drawing to display on a board above his stand. So striking was it that people walking by would stop to admire it and compare it with the real Pochetto and the real Doola begging on his hind legs. They stayed long enough to hear Pochetto's first haunting melodies and remained to hear the rest of his music and his quaint sounds.

That's where we shall leave the two of them Sam, happy with the swap they made that day in the square.

Now, before I go on with this packing up, what about a game while you're wearing the Pochetto coat? Let's find something to start you off.

Your coloured umbrella is still stuck in this pocket.

Ah yes, good. What have you seen me do with it?

I've seen you have trouble opening it. And then you've jerked it open and knocked off your false nose.

Right. Now see if you can think of something else to do with it.

Oh, I don't feel much like fun today.

Haven't I always said to you, that's the time a clown has to show that he's really a clown? Try for me, Sam. You'll make me feel better too.

Umm. I could hide something inside the umbrella.

Yes, yes you could.

And when I opened it, whatever was inside would fall over me.

71

Good. Now make out you've put it inside the umbrella. What could it be?

Some doves?

Yes.

Or some, some ping-pong balls?

That's more like it. Go on, parade around with the brolly full of ping-pong balls.

And I open it up like this. And they are trick balls. Some land on my nose, and I balance them there like this.

Fine.

And, they roll off one by one. And, I pretend to swallow them.

Great! That's even better. Keep going, Sam.

And . . .

About the Author

Ted Greenwood was born in Melbourne in 1930. For some years he worked as a school teacher and then in 1959 he graduated from RMIT in Fine Art (Painting) and became a lecturer in Art and Craft at Toorak State College. In 1968 he gave up his lecturing to devote time to writing and illustrating children's books.

Four of his six published picture books for children have won awards, and in 1972 he was given a Churchill Fellowship to travel to places of book and art interest, and to meet children in a variety of situations. Three of his books are published by Penguin: *Ginnie* (Kestrel), *VIP* and *Obstreperous* (both as Picture Puffins).

Ted Greenwood lives with his family in the Dandenong Mountains in Victoria.

ELMER THE RAT

Patrick Cook

Elmer was a rat, a very hungry rat, who lived on the Sydney water-front.

The seagulls (who thought they knew everything) told Elmer about The Other Place where there was always plenty to eat. But to reach it, Elmer had to stow away on a ship and scampered right into trouble.

Ships' rats with wicked teeth, sailors with boots and knives – they were all out to stop him. And The Other Place had a few shocks waiting for him too.

MAGPIE ISLAND

Colin Thiele

Magpie loved the wind and the steep, open sky over the Eyre Penin-
sula, which he roamed with his companions. One day a wedge-
tailed eagle came sailing out of the Nullarbor. Unable to resist
following the eagle, Magpie is seized by the strong north wind and
blown far out to sea. When eventually, he lands it is on a gaunt,
windswept, solitary island, and Magpie finds himself among thou-
sands of strange sea birds . . .

THE FURTHER ADVENTURES OF DR A.A.A. McGURK, M.D.

Osmar White
Illustrated by Jeff Hook

In these pages you will travel with the bravest explorer of modern times, the great Alastair Angus Archibald McGurk and his remarkable double-humped riding camel Cathie Khan whom he teaches to ski so that together they can search for the fabled Pole of Impossibility.

You will also meet a courageous hairy dog Trotsky, and a wandering band of displaced animals led by a refugee from the over-crowded tourist slopes of Mount Everest.

Why had they all gone to the ends of the earth? Were they to survive trial by blizzard, fire and icequake?

Or were they swallowed up by a yawning crevasse or a fuming fumarole?

HEARD ABOUT THE PUFFIN CLUB?

... it's a way of finding out more about Puffin books and authors, of winning prizes (in competitions), sharing jokes, a secret code, and perhaps seeing your name in print! When you join you get a copy of our magazine, *Puffin Post*, sent to you four times a year a badge and a membership book.

For details of subscription and an application form, send a stamped addressed envelope to:

The Puffin Club Dept A
Penguin Books Limited
Bath Road
Harmondsworth
Middlesex UB7 ODA

and if you live in Australia, for a copy of *Puffinalia* please write to

The Australian Puffin Club
Penguin Books Australia Limited
P.O. Box 257
Ringwood
Victoria 3134